2012 GREATEST Country Hits

PIANO • VOCAL • GUITAR

★ DELUXE ANNUAL EDITION ★ THE BIGGEST HITS ★ THE GREATEST ARTISTS

CONTENTS

Produced by
Alfred Music Publishing Co., Inc.
P.O. Box 10003
Van Nuys, CA 91410-0003
alfred.com

Printed in USA.

ISBN-10: 0-7390-8922-6
ISBN-13: 978-0-7390-8922-4

2012 2012

AS YOU TURN AWAY

Words and Music by
DAVE HAYWOOD, CHARLES KELLEY,
HILLARY SCOTT and MONTY POWELL

Slowly ♩ = 63

(with pedal)

Verse 1:

Female:

1. Stand-in' face___ to face,___ wrapped in your___ em - brace,___ I don't wan-na let you go, but you're al - read - y gone.___

BANJO

Words and Music by
WENDELL MOBLEY, TONY MARTIN
and NEIL THRASHER

Moderate country rock ♩ = 96

Banjo- 8 - 1

air and B___ S get too thick, can't take a breath_with-out get - tin' sick. I've

had e - nough_ of this con - crete jun - gle.___ 2. I drop my

Verses 2 (sing 2nd time only)

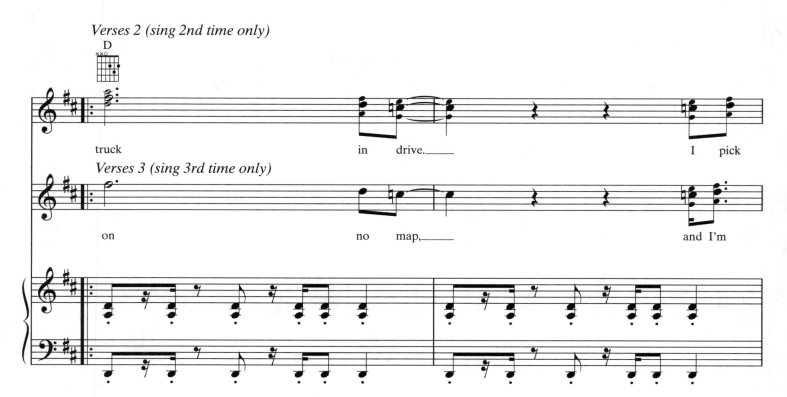

truck in drive.___ I pick

Verses 3 (sing 3rd time only)

on no map,___ and I'm

Chorus:

cross a few creeks and a cou-ple lit-tle shacks. (Whoa._____)

Four-wheel drive when you run out of road.

(Whoa._____)

And you go, and you go, and you go, 'til you hear that, 'til you hear that, 'til you hear that

ban - jo._____

Repeat ad lib. and fade

HOME

Words and Music by
BRETT BEAVERS, DIERKS BENTLEY
and DAN WILSON

Moderately ♩ = 120

Verse 1 & 4:

1. West, on a plane___ bound west___ I see___ her stretch - ing out
4. Brave, got - ta call___ it brave___ to chase___ that dream___ a - cross

* *Original recording in B, guitars tuned down 1/2 step.*

Chorus:

1.2. From the moun - tains high, to the wave -
3. Been a long, hard ride, got a ways__

crashed coast. There's a way_____ to
to go. This is still_____ the

find better days_____ I know. Been a long,__
place that we all_____ call home. Been a long,__

__ hard ride, got a ways_____ to
__ hard ride, and I won't_____ lose

To Coda ⊕
(sing harmony cue
2nd and 3rd times)

go.
But this is still_____ the place that we all_____

hope.
But this is still_____ the place place that we all_____

1.

_____ call home.

2.

_____ call

Bridge:

home.
Whoa,_____ yeah._____

CRAZY GIRL

Words and Music by
LEE BRICE and LIZ ROSE

Moderately slow, in "one" ♩. = 54

Guitar Capo 2 → D

Piano → E

(with pedal)

Verse:
Bm
C#m

1. Ba - by, why you wan - na cry? __ You real - ly ought - a know that I __
2. I would - n't last a sin - gle day, __ I'd prob - 'bly just fade a - way. __

Crazy Girl - 6 - 2

DANCIN' AWAY WITH MY HEART

Words and Music by
DAVE HAYWOOD, CHARLES KELLEY,
HILLARY SCOTT and JOSH KEAR

32

DIRT ROAD ANTHEM

Words and Music by
BRANTLEY GILBERT and COLT FORD

Slow country blues feel ♩ = 63

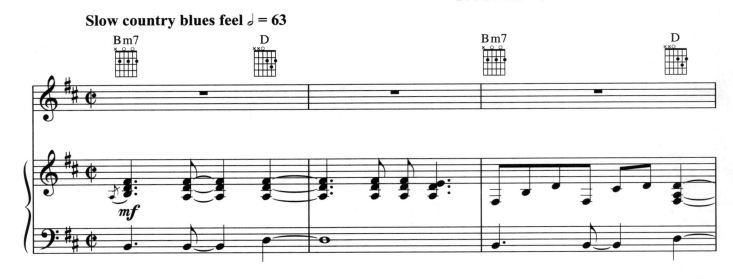

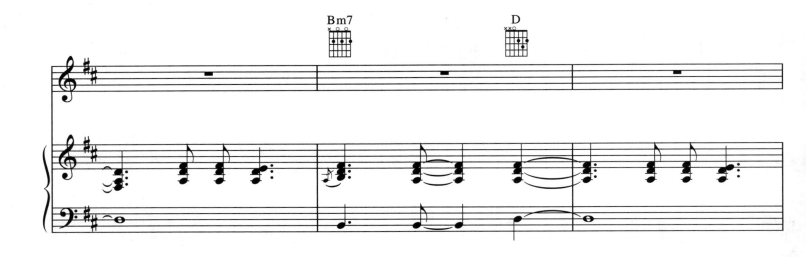

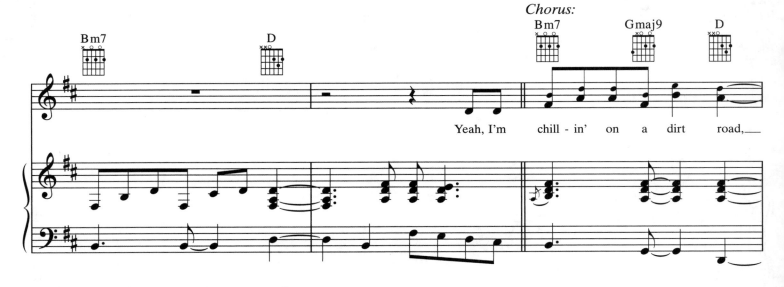

Chorus:

Yeah, I'm chill-in' on a dirt road,

Dirt Road Anthem - 8 - 1

Verse 2:
I sit back and think about them good ol' days,
The way we were raised, and our southern ways.
And we like cornbread, and biscuits,
And if it's broke, 'round here we fix it.
I can take ya'll where ya need to go,
Down to my hood, back in them woods.
We do it different 'round here, that's right,
But we sure do it good, and we do it all night.
See, if you really wanna know how it feels
To get off the road with trucks and four wheels,
Jump on in and, man, tell your friends,
We'll raise some hell where the blacktop ends.
(To Chorus:)

HONEY BEE

Words and Music by
BEN HAYSLIP and RHETT AKINS

1. Girl, I been think-in' 'bout us, and you know I ain't good at this stuff,
3. Your kiss just said it all.___ I'm___ glad___ we had___ this talk.

Honey Bee - 8 - 1

Chorus 1 & 3:

Chorus 2:

You'll be my hon-ey-suck-le; I'll be your hon - ey bee.___

(Guitar solo ad lib....

I DON'T WANT THIS NIGHT TO END

Words and Music by
BEN HAYSLIP, LUKE BRYAN,
DALLAS DAVIDSON and RHETT AKINS

Moderately ♩ = 112

1. Girl, I know I don't_ know you, but your pret-ty lit-tle eyes_ so blue are pull-ing__ me in like the
cuss the morn-ing when_ it comes, 'cause I know that the ris - ing sun ain't no good_ for me, 'cause

I Don't Want This Night to End - 6 - 1

Chorus:

I LOVE YOU THIS BIG

Words and Music by
RONNIE JACKSON, BRETT JAMES,
ESTER DEAN and JAY SMITH

I Love You This Big - 8 - 1

but I know_ how I_____ feel._____

I'll love you all the time._____

I might not have_ too much ex - pe - ri - ence,

Deep - er than_ the o - cean_

but I know when love_ is real

and high - er than_ the pines._____

try. I love you this_ big._

Bridge:

try. I love you this big,_____ so much big-

ger than__ I ev - er dreamed_my heart_____ ev - er_____ would._

___ I love you this big,_____ and I'd write_

IF I DIE YOUNG

Words and Music by
KIMBERLY PERRY

Slowly ♩ = 69   *Chorus:*

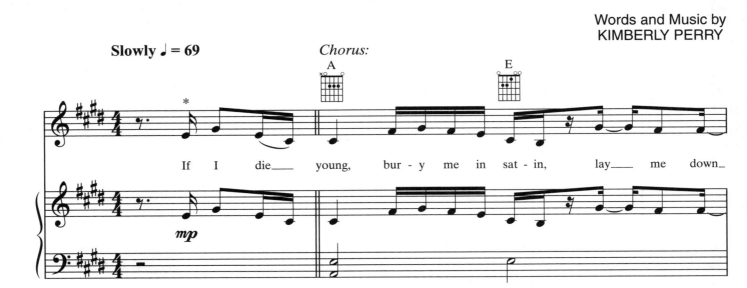

If I die____ young, bur-y me in sat-in, lay____ me down____

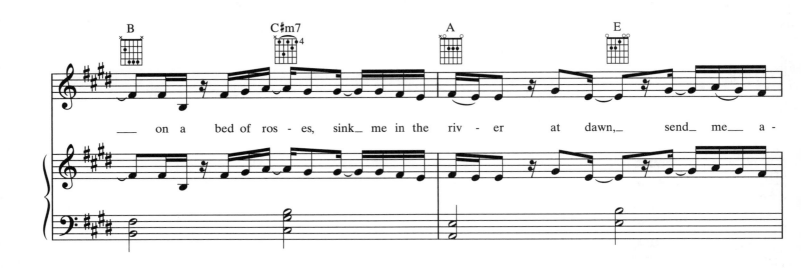

____ on a bed of ros-es, sink__ me in the riv-er at dawn,__ send__ me__ a-

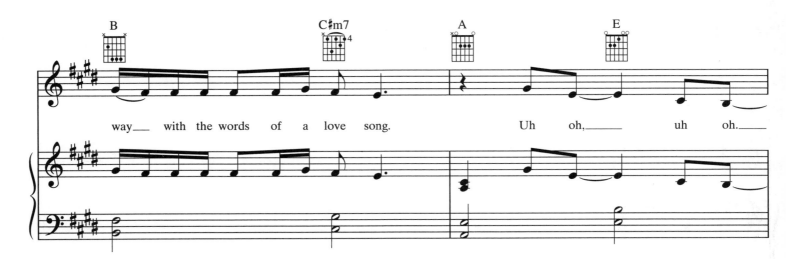

way____ with the words of a love song.   Uh oh,_____ uh oh.____

*All vocals written at pitch.

If I Die Young - 8 - 1

Verse 3:

What I nev-er did is done. 3. A pen-ny for my thoughts, oh no,___ I'll sell___ them for a dol-lar.

They're worth so much more af - ter I'm a gon - er. And___

may - be then you'll hear the words___ I've been sing - ing.

Fun - ny, when you're dead how peo - ple start___ lis - t'nin'.___

I'M GONNA LOVE YOU THROUGH IT

Words and Music by
BEN HAYSLIP, JIMMY YEARY
and SONYA ISAACS

*Guitars tuned down 1 whole step.

I'm Gonna Love You Through It - 5 - 1

*Play chords in parenthesis 2nd time.

MY KINDA PARTY

Words and Music by
BRANTLEY GILBERT

JUST A KISS

Words and Music by
CHARLES KELLEY, DAVE HAYWOOD,
HILLARY SCOTT and DALLAS DAVIDSON

Moderately slow ♩ = 72

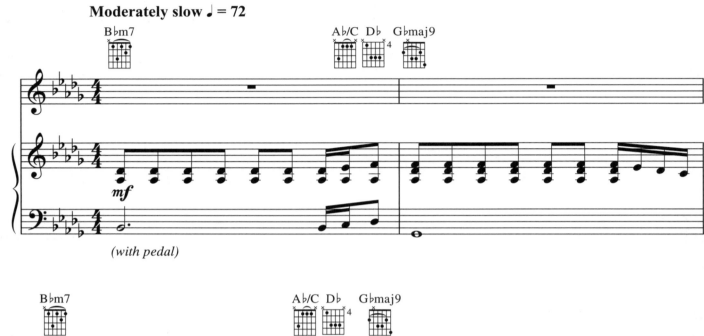

Verse 1:

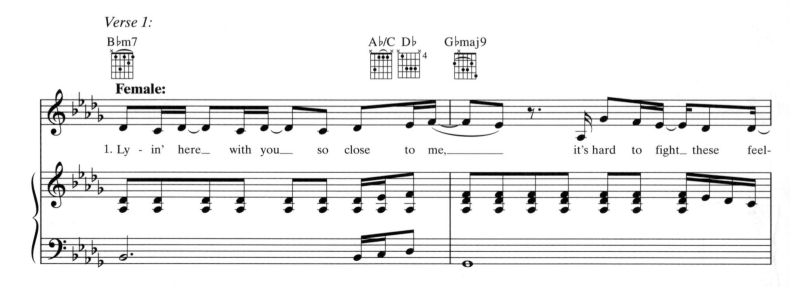

1. Ly-in' here___ with you___ so close to me,_____ it's hard to fight___ these feel-

⊕ *Coda*

LOVE DON'T RUN

Words and Music by
JOE LEATHERS, BEN GLOVER
and RACHEL THIBODEAU

Slowly ♩ = 76

Verse 1:

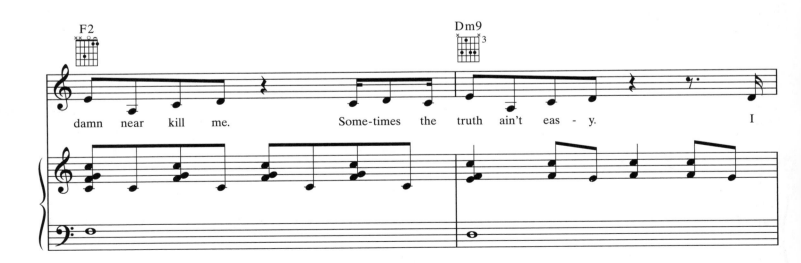

Love Don't Run - 8 - 1

Verse 2:

MY HEART CAN'T TELL YOU NO

Words and Music by
DENNIS MORGAN and SIMON CLIMIE

My Heart Can't Tell You No - 6 - 1

My Heart Can't Tell You No - 6 - 5

My Heart Can't Tell You No - 6 - 6

REALITY

Words and Music by
BRETT JAMES and
KENNY CHESNEY

Verse 1 (sing 1st time only):

1. For me,___ it's a beach bar, or on a boat un-der-neath the stars,___

Verse 2 (sing 2nd time only):

___ some days,___ it's a bitch, it's a bum-mer. We need a rock and roll show in the sum-mer

*Play C/E 2nd time.

Reality - 6 - 2

Yeah,_____ oh,____ yeah._____

Come on___ ev - 'ry - bod - y, break__ free._____

Come on___ ev - 'ry - bod - y, break__ free._____

RED SOLO CUP

Words and Music by
BRETT BEAVERS, JIM BEAVERS,
BRAD WARREN and BRETT WARREN

Chorus:

Red so- lo cup, I fill you up; let's have a par- ty, let's have a par- ty. I love you red so- lo cup. I lift you up; pro- ceed to par- ty, pro- ceed to par- ty.

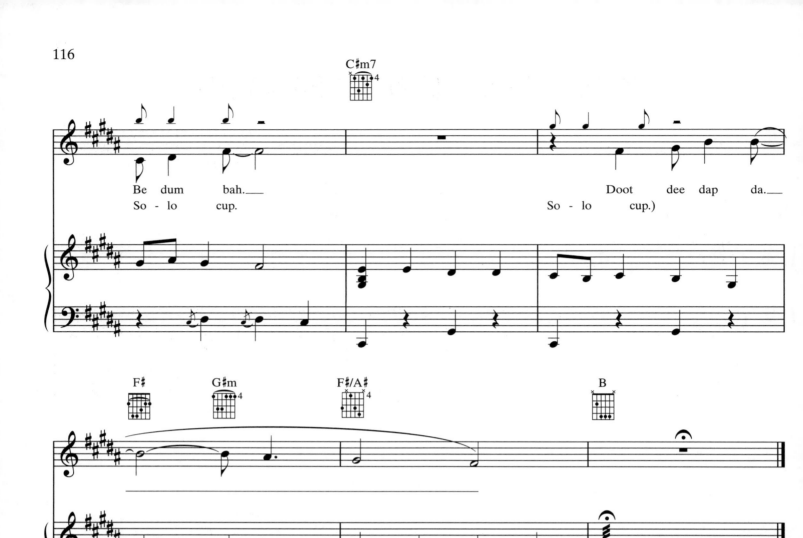

Spoken:

Verse 2:
Now, I really love how you're easy to stack.
But I really hate how you're easy to crack,
'Cause when beer runs down in front of my pack,
Well, that, my friends is quite yucky.
But I have to admit that the ladies get smitten
Admirin' how sharply my first name is written
On you with a Sharpie when I get to hittin'
On them to help me get lucky.
(To Chorus:)

THREATEN ME WITH HEAVEN

Threaten Me With Heaven - 7 - 1

SHE WON'T BE LONELY LONG

Words and Music by
DOUG JOHNSON, PHIL O'DONNELL
and GALEN GRIFFIN

She Won't Be Lonely Long - 6 - 1

Bridge:

If I had a wom-an like that,__ man, I'd__ let her know. I'd hold her tight. I'd hold her close, do ev-'ry-thing, do an-y-thing to let her know she'd nev-er ev-er be a-lone.__

(Inst. solo ad lib....

She Won't Be Lonely Long - 6 - 4

SMILE

Words and Music by
MATTHEW SHAFER, BLAIR DALY,
J.T. HARDING and JEREMY BOSE

Smile - 6 - 1

Verses 1 (cont.) & 2:

TEMPORARY HOME

Words and Music by
CARRIE UNDERWOOD, LUKE LAIRD
and ZAC MALOY

Temporary Home - 6 - 1

Chorus:

this was just__ a stop__ on the way to where__I'm go - ing.__ I'm not a - fraid__

be - cause__ I know__ this was my__ tem - po - rar -

y home.__ Mm.

This is our tem-po-rar - y home.__

WALK ME DOWN THE MIDDLE

Words and Music by
KIMBERLY PERRY, NEIL PERRY
and REID PERRY

Chorus:

WE OWNED THE NIGHT

Words and Music by
DAVE HAYWOOD, CHARLES KELLEY
and DALLAS DAVIDSON

1. Tell me, have you ev - er want - ed some - one so much it hurts?

*Original recording in C♯ with Guitar tuned down a half step.

We Owned the Night - 7 - 1

Bridge:

YOU AND TEQUILA

Words and Music by
DEANA CARTER and MATRACA BERG

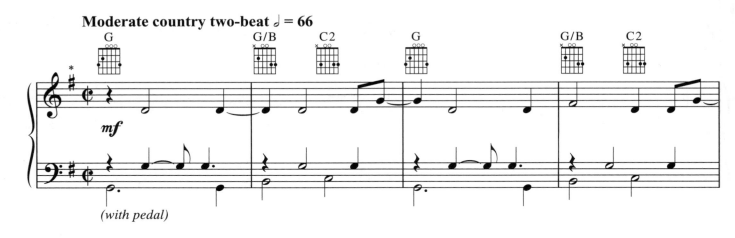

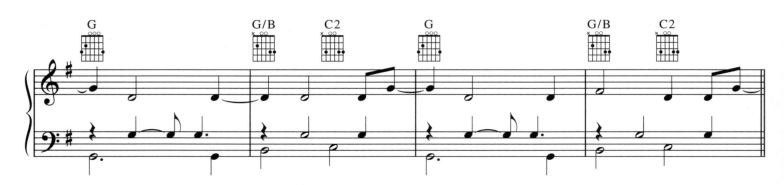

Verse 1 (sing 1st time only):

1. Ba-by, here I am a-gain,__ kick-in' dust__ in the Can-yon wind,

Verse 2 (sing 2nd time only):

2. Thir-ty days and thir-ty nights, been put-tin' up a real good fight,

*Original recording in F♯ major, Guitar tuned down 1/2 step.

You and Tequila - 6 - 1

160

that do___ you in.___

(Inst. solo ad lib....

D.S. % al Coda

...end solo)

WHY WAIT

Words and Music by
JIMMY YEARY, NEIL THRASHER
and TOM SHAPIRO

Why Wait - 7 - 1